F

Buddy BOOKS

Prehistoric Animals

Scimitar Cat

ABDO
Publishing Company

A Buddy Book
by
Michael P. Goecke

VISIT US AT
www.abdopub.com

Published by Buddy Books, an imprint of ABDO Publishing Company, 4940 Viking Drive, Edina, Minnesota 55435. Copyright © 2004 by Abdo Consulting Group, Inc. International copyrights reserved in all countries. No part of this book may be reproduced in any form without written permission from the publisher.

Printed in the United States.

Edited by: Christy DeVillier
Contributing Editor: Matt Ray
Graphic Design: Deborah Coldiron
Image Research: Deborah Coldiron
Illustrations: Deborah Coldiron, Denise Esner
Photographs: Corel, Eyewire, Steve McHugh, Photodisc

Library of Congress Cataloging-in-Publication Data

Goecke, Michael P., 1968-
    Scimitar cat / Michael P. Goecke.
      p. cm. — (Prehistoric animals. Set II)
    Summary: Introduces the physical characteristics, habitat, and behavior of this prehistoric relative of modern-day big cats, such as the lion, cheetah, and leopard.
    Includes bibliographical references and index.
    ISBN 1-57765-977-5
    1. Scimitar cat—Juvenile literature. [1. Scimitar cat. 2. Mammals, Fossil. 3. Prehistoric animals. 4. Paleontology.] I. Title.

QE882.C15 G644 2003
569'.755—dc21

2002032274

Table of Contents

Prehistoric Animals 4

The Scimitar Cat 6

What It Looked Like 8

Deadly Hunter 13

Prides And Dens 16

Scimitar Cat's World 18

Fossils 21

Important Words 23

Web Sites 23

Index 24

Prehistoric Animals

People began writing about 5,500 years ago. This marked the end of prehistoric times.

Many exciting animals lived in prehistoric times. There were saber-toothed cats, woolly mammoths, and giant apes. These prehistoric animals are not around today. Scientists study bones and other fossils to learn about these exciting animals.

Prehistoric Animals

5

The Scimitar Cat

Scimitar cat

(SIH-muh-tar cat)

There are more than 35 kinds of saber-toothed cats. They are famous for their large, knife-like teeth.

Some saber-toothed cats were built like bears. Others looked more like cheetahs. These cheetah-like cats are called scimitar cats.

Scimitar cats lived in many places throughout the world. They had sharp "scimitar" teeth. A scimitar is a curved sword.

7

What It Looked Like

Scimitar cats were about the size of lions. They probably grew to become as heavy as 200 pounds (91 kg).

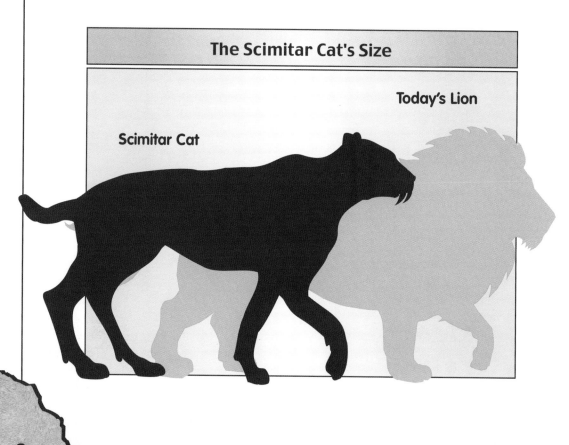

The Scimitar Cat's Size

Today's Lion

Scimitar Cat

The scimitar cat was named for
its large canine teeth.

9

A scimitar cat had a light body with slim bones. Like a cheetah, it had long front legs. Its back legs were shorter. The scimitar cat's tail was short like a bobcat's tail.

The scimitar cat had a short tail like this bobcat's tail.

The scimitar cat's two big canine teeth were curved. They curved downward from the cat's upper jaw. These teeth could grow to become four inches (ten cm) long. Like a steak knife, these teeth had small, sharp points. These points made the scimitar cat's teeth very sharp.

All saber-toothed cats had large canine teeth.

Fun Facts

Fast Cats

Cheetahs are the fastest cats in the world. They can run as fast as 70 miles (113 km) per hour. Cheetahs have non-retractable claws. Non-retractable claws stay out all the time. They help cheetahs grip the ground as they run.

Scientists believe the scimitar cat was a fast runner, too. It had non-retractable claws on its back feet. Maybe this prehistoric cat ran as fast as 60 miles (97 km) per hour.

Cheetah

Scimitar Cat

Deadly Hunter

The scimitar cat was a predator. It may have hunted young mastodons and mammoths. Mastodons and mammoths were prehistoric elephants. They had tough skin. The scimitar cat probably used its sharp canine teeth to kill these tough-skinned animals.

Scimitar cats may have been daytime hunters like today's cheetahs.

Many of today's cats hunt at night. Cheetahs are different. They hunt during the day. Some scientists believe scimitar cats hunted during the day, too.

The scimitar cat probably stalked its prey. Stalking cats quietly sneak up behind animals. This helps them catch prey by surprise.

This cheetah may be stalking its prey.

Prides And Dens

Today's lions live in groups, or prides. They sometimes work together to kill prey. Lions share food with pride members. Maybe scimitar cats lived in prides, too.

A pride of lions.

This bobcat is using a cave as its den.

Today's cats often raise their cubs in dens. A den is a hidden place. Scientists believe scimitar cats used dens, too. They probably raised their cubs in caves.

Scientists have names for important time periods in Earth's history. Scimitar cats lived during a time period called the Pleistocene. The Pleistocene began about two million years ago.

A Geologic Timeline
248 Million Years Ago – Today

Triassic 248 – 213 Million Years Ago	Jurassic 213 – 145 Million Years Ago	Cretaceous 145 – 65 Million Years Ago	Paleocene 65 – 56 Million Years Ago	Eocene 56 – 34 Million Years Ago	Oligocene 34 – 24 Million Years Ago	Miocene 24 – 5 Million Years Ago	Pliocene 5 – 2 Million Years Ago	Pleistocene 2 Million – 11,500 Years Ago	Holocene 11,500 Years Ago – Today

Age Of Dinosaurs 248 – 65 Million Years Ago	Age Of Mammals 65 Million Years Ago – Today

Scimitar cats lived between two million and 10,000 years ago.

The Pleistocene World

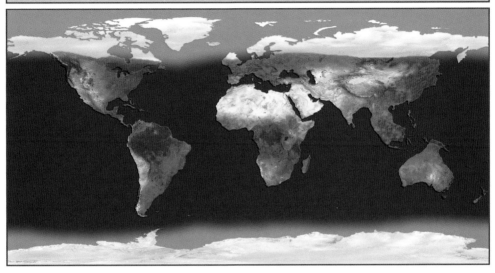

Ice covered parts of the world during the Pleistocene.

The last Ice Age took place during the Pleistocene. During that time, the world cooled. Giant sheets of ice covered many lands. Woolly mammoths, giant sloths, dire wolves, and rhinos lived during the Ice Age, too.

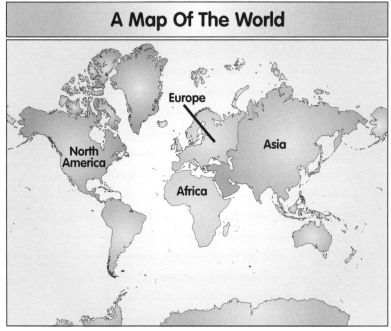

A Map Of The World

Europe

North America

Asia

Africa

Scimitar cat fossils have been found in North America, Europe, Africa, and Asia.

Many animals died out near the end of the Ice Age. A sudden climate change may have killed them. Some of these animals may have been the scimitar cat's prey. Did the scimitar cat die out because its prey disappeared? No one is sure.

Fossils

Fossils are important. Scientists study fossils to learn about prehistoric animals.

Georges Cuvier was a French scientist. He studied some tooth fossils found in France. He wrote about them in 1824. He thought the large teeth belonged to a bear. Other scientists thought the same teeth came from a dinosaur.

This boy is holding a fossil from a large saber-toothed cat.

In 1833, a scientist named Johann Jakob Kaup studied the same tooth fossils. He decided they belonged to a cat. Kaup was right. The fossils were teeth from a scimitar cat.

Important Words

canine teeth sharp and pointed teeth. Most animals have four canine teeth.

climate the weather of a place over time.

fossil remains of very old animals and plants commonly found in the ground. A fossil can be a bone, a footprint, or any trace of life.

Ice Age a period in Earth's history when ice covered parts of the world. The last Ice Age ended about 11,500 years ago.

predator an animal that hunts and eats other animals.

prehistoric describes anything that was around more than 5,500 years ago.

prey an animal that is food for another animal.

stalk to secretly follow prey.

Web Sites

To learn more about scimitar cats, visit ABDO Publishing Company on the World Wide Web. Web sites about scimitar cats are featured on our Book Links page. These links are routinely monitored and updated to provide the most current information available.

www.abdopub.com

Index

Africa 20

Asia 20

bear 7, 21

bobcat 10, 17

canine teeth 9, 11, 13

caves 17

cheetah...........7, 10, 12, 14, 15

climate 20

Cuvier, Georges.....................21

den 17

dinosaur.......................18, 21

dire wolves 19

Europe................................20

fossils 4, 20, 21, 22

France 21

giant apes............................4

giant sloths 19

Ice Age 19, 20

Kaup, Johann Jakob 22

lions 8, 16

mammoths 4, 13, 19

mastodons 13

non-retractable claws...........12

North America 20

Pleistocene.....................18, 19

predator.............................13

prey 15, 16, 20

pride...................................16

rhinos.................................19

saber-toothed cats........4, 6, 7, 11, 22

stalk..................................15